Effective Habits
of a Newborn
Christian

TINA TOGUCHI

WESTBOW
PRESS®
A DIVISION OF THOMAS NELSON
& ZONDERVAN

WestBow Press books may be ordered through booksellers or by contacting:

WestBow Press
A Division of Thomas Nelson & Zondervan
1663 Liberty Drive
Bloomington, IN 47403
www.westbowpress.com
1 (866) 928-1240

ISBN: 978-1-9736-0100-5 (sc)
ISBN: 978-1-9736-0099-2 (e)

Library of Congress Control Number: 2017913513

Print information available on the last page.

WestBow Press rev. date: 09/08/2017

PREFACE

Writing a book can be a daunting experience, especially when the subject involves sharing one's Christian values and beliefs. Nonetheless, I experienced a similar challenge when I entered a new church. Without a firm grounding, it was difficult for me to find counselors who could help me with understanding the basic steps in my growth as a new Christian. The advice I received was, "Find a good local church, and start reading the Bible. It will give you all you need to know." However, not having a personal guide to learn about the Christian walk made learning a bit challenging. With this experience, I became motivated to put pen to paper and to impart what I have learned over the years. God has truly been an amazing inspiration to open my eyes to the possibilities involved with a closer walk with him.

In this endeavor, I want to give God all of the glory in the publication of this book. Simply put, I could not have done this without God. Completing this book was supernatural. He gave me all of the key ideas, such as the title, the chapters, the habits, and the examples. Without his clear direction and firm encouragement, I could never have finished this work on time.

I would like to thank my husband, Bob, for his inspiration and both of my children, Paula Church and Jessica Wamsley, for their faith and encouragement that assisted me in the writing of this book. They have truly been the wind beneath my wings as I have worked to complete this project.

INTRODUCTION

New Christians need a place to start. Whoever is new in the Christian faith is basically an outsider in a brand-new field of personal exploration, growth, and lifelong development. Oftentimes reaching out to the elderly or experienced members in a church can be challenging and a very difficult experience. Where does the new Christian go for advice? Looking around your past also can be challenging; since your old friends are not necessarily interested in starting a new walk. In essence, being a new Christian, at times, can be a lonely experience. Who can you trust to provide the answers to your heartfelt questions? This book is designed just for you. Read on, and you will truly enjoy what you find.

The Effective Habits of a Newborn Christian helps those who have not found a mentor to becoming a Christian. You don't have to meet anyone to get started; you can begin to read about Christian habits that are effective until you meet the right person for a mentor. It gets into the very basics of effective habits that have worked for countless others who have begun the walk. It can also serve as a good guide for those young teenagers who have started an early walk with the Lord but perhaps are not ready for a one-on-one counseling relationship. To others who are already mature in the Christian faith, this book can serve as a refresher to help polish those habits that endure long after the initial motivation wears off.

Develop the Habit of Establishing a Relationship

ONE OF THE MOST EFFECTIVE habits that a new Christian can develop is to begin a relationship with the God of the universe. Above all, this habit will sustain you when the going gets tough as a new Christian. It also will sustain you when you've lost that initial burst of energy and the tremendous inspiration that accompanied you when you became born again. Long after your friends stop talking about the Lord, long after your baptism, and long after your born-again experience, this important habit will endure and stay with you. Without a doubt, establishing a relationship with the one and only God is a habit that is worth investing in.

How do you develop a relationship? Not surprisingly, a relationship with God is, in many ways, similar to developing a relationship with a close friend. Some of the basics include learning to spend time with God, getting to know everything about him, seeking him for who he is, learning to hear his voice, making a lifelong commitment to him, and learning to trust and rely on him. Relationships take time. Relationships are an investment in someone you truly care about. Relationships are important in developing a two-way pathway of care and concern for a lifelong partner.

The key to a great relationship is not to give up. New Christians often hear about the Lord, get motivated for a season, and then slowly stop working on this relationship. The worries of life are frequent inhibitors of this great habit of relationship. The worries of life can come in many forms. First, your job or series of jobs start to require more and more of your time. Your boss places more commitments on you, sales orders start to increase, and your fellow workers expect you to show up earlier and to leave later and later each day. Second, friends, family members, and loved ones begin to make more demands on your spare time. The deluge of dinner outings, parties, social engagements, softball games, barbecues, and the like seem to increase in frequency and length. Third, your volunteer organizations start to require more of your personal attention. Weekly club meetings, new leadership positions, fund-raisers, weekend pancake breakfasts, and a host of other commitments begin to pop up out of seemingly nowhere. Don't fret. As a new Christian, you must realize that the world will begin to push back. The environment of the world will make it more and more challenging to spend time as a Christian. You must develop habits to endure this onslaught and to continue in the walk with the Lord.

Set time aside each day to develop your relationship with the Lord. Whether it is the first thirty minutes each morning, your daily commute to work, your twenty-minute break in the workday, a short break during lunch, or your return commute to your home, you can find time each day to spend on your relationship with the Lord. At first you will have the feeling that nothing is happening. This is a normal experience. Relationships take commitment. Be sure to invest in your relationship with the Lord, and over time, he will begin to respond to your commitment. For some this may be two weeks, and for others it may take a month. Nonetheless, rest assured—the Lord of the universe will respond to your daily commitment to spend time with him.

The Habit of Forgiveness

THIS HABIT IS ASSOCIATED WITH putting first things first. Before we can even consider getting close to God, we must first apply the habit of forgiveness to get right in the sight of God. You may ask, "Why do I need to ask for forgiveness?" It gets to one of God's foundational requirements, and this is how we establish a right standing with God—before God can forgive us of our sins.

Jesus gave advice to his disciples that forgiveness of others is a requirement before the Father can forgive us of our sins. He stated in Mark 11:25–26, "Whenever you stand praying, if you have anything against anyone, forgive him, that your Father in heaven may also forgive you your trespasses. But *if you do not forgive, neither will your Father in heaven forgive your trespasses*" (my emphasis). We must remember that unforgiveness can be the primary obstacle that prevents our prayers from being answered. All scripture quotations in this book are taken from the _____ version of the Bible, unless otherwise noted

How many times are we expected to forgive? In the book of Matthew 18:21–22, the apostle Peter asked Jesus, "Lord, how often shall my brother sin against me, and I forgive him? Up to seven times?" Seven would appear to be a logical number.

Yet Jesus wanted to emphasize the importance of forgiveness and told Peter, "I do not say to you, up to seven times, but up to seventy times seven."

Seventy times seven? That would equal 490 times! Wow! That would take considerable patience and time. The point is that Jesus wants to emphasize the criticality of forgiveness if we want to receive God's forgiveness for our sins.

MAKE A LIST

To help you identify all those who have offended you and require your forgiveness, I recommend that you write a list. Identify all of those individuals who have hurt you, list the reason they hurt you, and ask God to help you to remember all of those individuals. If you truly feel anger and resentment, this is probably because you have allowed this unforgiveness to build up over many years—and in some cases, you may have forgotten who has wronged you, and you don't understand where the anger and resentment comes from. God can help you to remember and to confess your forgiveness of these individuals. *The only person who suffers from unforgiveness … is you.* It basically seems unfair, but it is the only way for you to escape from your chains. Just try it, and you will be truly surprised by the waves of forgiveness that God will bring to your life. You will feel the burden lifted, and you will start to feel the freshness of freedom and salvation. All of this may sound supernatural—but Jesus is real. The experience of lifting your life's burdens will happen; just believe and trust God.

THE PRICE OF UNFORGIVENESS

Personal bondage is the result of unforgiveness.

Remember: unless you can get through this obstacle of

unforgiveness, you can never get to the point where God begins to answer your prayers. When you wonder why God doesn't answer your prayers, go back to Effective Habit #2 and start to forgive all of those who have hurt you—and include major hurts, such as personal betrayal, family violence, rape, murder, false accusations, false imprisonment, and those things we cannot even discuss in public. Also, forgive those who have hurt you in minor ways, such those who have hurt you with gossip, slander, and unfair criticism. In the end, forgiveness benefits you in far more ways than you can imagine, as it restores your relationship with the God of the universe.

Learn to Read the Living Word

SPENDING TIME READING THE BIBLE is a critical habit to establish with the Lord. The Bible is your beginner's handbook to learning about the Christian lifestyle. Everything you need to know is in there. God, in his infinite wisdom, ensured that an instruction book was provided through the generations for anyone who is willing to read his Word. The history of God's walk with humankind, the basic rules of Christian living, personal stories of successful Christians, indications of what it takes to succeed with the Lord, what to do when you have setbacks, and a basic understanding of God's enduring love and mercy for you are all direct benefits of reading God's Word.

ASK THE LORD FOR HELP IN READING HIS WORD

During my early walk with the Lord, I found it very difficult to read the Bible. Distractions would pop up. Unexpected phone calls, unscheduled visits, unpleasant e-mails, and a host of other nuisances would emerge when I was trying to read the Word. If the distractions didn't stop me, then the next thing I felt was something trying to make me sleep. Tiredness, weariness, heaviness, and sleepiness would all creep up on me and would make it extremely difficult to read. More often than not, the sleepiness would do me in to prevent me from reading the Bible. I found the sleepiness difficult to resist. A third challenge was that parts of the Bible would become very difficult to understand due to the context of the story. Books like Jeremiah, Isaiah, or Ezekiel were challenging to read due to their complexity. Without a doubt, you will have initial challenges in reading the Word, but if you gain the habit of regularly spending time in the Word, then it will get easier and easier. I can guarantee you that over time, you will grow to love reading the Bible. Moreover, you will begin to experience new revelations and new blessings each time you dwell in the Word.

SAY A SHORT PRAYER TO THE LORD TO MAKE IT EASIER

I found that praying before reading is key to a successful experience. God is a listener. Before starting your time in the Word, ask God to provide you with the Holy Spirit to help you to understand what he wants you to get out of the Word. Learn to let the Holy Spirit lead you to the right book to read. Second, pray for the Lord to protect you during your prayer time. Ask him to remove or reduce all possible distractions so that your time in the Word may be fruitful and meet God's expectations.

SET A CERTAIN TIME EACH DAY TO READ THE WORD

Habits are formed through regular routine. I find that when I designate a time each day with the Bible, I generally keep my promise to read the Word. If setting aside time for reading is challenging, consider playing recordings of the books of the Bible during your commute. Many of us have hour-long commutes, and you can cover a lot of the Bible during an hour in the Word. Another technique that I have used is to play a Bible CD when I am showering and doing my hair in the morning. At times, when I don't have a CD, I connect my smartphone to a free Bible audio link and am able to hear entire books of the Bible free, over the Internet. I easily manage to spend thirty minutes and longer listening to the Word each morning in the bathroom. With a little bit of thought, we all can find innovative ways to spend time in the Word each day.

GOD'S WORD HAS POWER

The manifestation of this power is developed over time. As you spend more and more time in the Word, this power will emerge after long-term commitment. Nothing happens overnight. Patience and dedication are required. With this commitment, reading certain words of the Bible can and will give you a renewed burst of energy. Isaiah 40:28–31 comes to mind. Over time, when I read these verses, I receive a boost of power. It states,

> Hast thou not known? Hast thou not heard, that the everlasting God, the LORD, the Creator of the ends of the earth, fainteth not, neither is weary? There is no searching of his understanding. He giveth power to the faint; and to them that have no might he increaseth strength. Even the youths shall faint and be weary, and the young men shall utterly fall: But they that wait upon the LORD shall renew their strength; they shall mount up with wings as eagles; they shall run, and not be weary; and they shall walk, and not faint.

Tina Toguchi

READING GOD'S WORD IS AN IMPORTANT HABIT TO GET TO KNOW ABOUT GOD

To many, the ways of the Lord are hidden. Spending time in the Word is similar to finding hidden treasure, whenever we spend time with God. For me, it opens my eyes by sharing with me unique secrets about the Lord. I discovered through the Bible that King David had a heart like God's. I asked, what does that mean? By reading the books of 1 Samuel, 2 Samuel, and 1 Kings, I began to realize that David had a unique heart. He was bold and he was courageous, yet he was also extremely merciful and forgave his enemies regularly. Of note, his predecessor, King Saul, hunted David for eight years across Israel, yet after all of this, David forgave King Saul. Additionally, David's son Absalom tried to kill him for the kingdom, and David forgave them. David was even merciful toward King Saul's descendants, despite the king's ridiculously harsh treatment of David under his rule.

EFFECTIVE HABIT #4

The Habit of Firsts

ONE OF THE HABITS THAT God truly appreciates is the habit of firsts. The habit of firsts is not just a simple step to get us started, and it is definitely not temporary or fleeting in nature. The habit of firsts becomes a recurring way of putting "first things first" and is a lifelong habit that incorporates all of our thoughts, our words, our deeds, and our actions. It is a driver of behavior in all that we do.

The habit of firsts means that we learn how to put God first. While it may be simple in principle, it can be somewhat challenging to start this habit. For example, how many of us start each morning by making God the first person we talk to? Do we open our eyes when it is still dark and say, "Good morning, Holy Spirit"? Then, how many of us have the habit of walking straight to our quiet place and beginning the day with prayer to set conditions for the entire day.

Our hearts are important to God. Do we put God first in our hearts, above all things? If we truly are committed to the Christian lifestyle, then putting God first in our hearts is a basic expectation. To place this idea in perspective, Jesus said in Matthew 13:45–46, "The kingdom of heaven is like a merchant seeking beautiful *pearls*, who, when he had found one *pearl of great price*, went and sold all that he had and bought it (emphasis mine)." Later in Matthew, Jesus repeated the expectation of the necessity of putting God first by saying, "And every one that hath forsaken houses, or brethren, or sisters, or father, or mother, or wife, or children, or lands, for my name's sake, shall receive an hundredfold, and shall inherit everlasting life" (Matthew 19:29). Without a doubt, God expects us to place him first in our hearts but reminds us that the rewards of this commitment are indeed great.

God expects us to place him first in our finances. The first fruits of our labor are mentioned in the book of Genesis. The basic habit is to give to God—through our local churches or charities—the very first amount of money, goods, or harvest that we receive in life. This is not always easy. It took me several years to get to the point where I was able to give the full tithe. Frequently, I gave what I could and made up the difference through community service for several years. Over time, I was able to make the full amount. Of note, Abraham, the early father of faith, was the first to display this habit and expectation by giving his tithes, or the first 10 percent of his goods, to God's representative, Methuselah, in Genesis 14:18–20. While this practice is actually quite challenging; you can rest assured that God will bless you as you fulfill this commitment.

God has given us promises if we place him first in our finances. Later, in Malachi 3:10, God reminds us,

> Bring ye all the tithes into the storehouse, that
> there may be meat in mine house, and prove me
> now herewith, saith the LORD of hosts, if I will
> not open you the windows of heaven, and pour
> you out a blessing, that there shall not be room

enough to receive it … And I will rebuke the devourer for your sakes, and he shall not destroy the fruits of your ground; neither shall your vine cast her fruit before the time in the field, saith the LORD of hosts … And all nations shall call you blessed: for ye shall be a delightsome land, saith the LORD of hosts.

Through experience, many can attest to God's goodness in blessing our finances as we place him first.

Praise and Worship—Creating the Atmosphere for Effective Prayer

THE VALUE OF PRAISE AND WORSHIP

THIS GETS BACK TO ESTABLISHING our habit of firsts. One of the first things we need to do in prayer is to sequence the most important things first. Generally, most people want to start asking God for favors right away. We are not patient. We really want to get after what God can do for us. It's generally all about us. Even the order in which we ask for things in prayer is an indication of our habits. To truly connect with God in prayer, we need to learn to think about God first. What would God want us to do in prayer? How can we best serve God by praying for those things that can advance his kingdom on earth? What prayers would make God encouraged with our relationship with him? Oftentimes, it is not about asking for selfish things first but establishing the relationship with him.

CREATING THE RIGHT ATMOSPHERE

When we approach the God of the universe, we must realize that there are certain things that could improve our relationship in prayer. It begins with the atmosphere. We must seek and find a private, quiet place to communicate with God. Privacy and quietness ensure that we will not be distracted by the business of life. Privacy also conveys an atmosphere of intimacy. Privacy means that this conversation is only between you and God. Nobody else needs to be involved. The right atmosphere could also include Christian music. I have found that playing quiet Christian music in the background truly enhances my prayer to God. God loves music. He really loves Christian music. You will find that Christian music creates the mood and serves to empower the Holy Spirit when we pray to God.

PLAY CHRISTIAN MUSIC

The earliest example of the power of Christian music is David's playing the harp to ward off evil spirits from afflicting King Saul. In 1 Samuel 16:23, scriptures reveal, "And it came to pass, when the evil spirit from God was upon Saul, that David took an harp, and played with his hand: so Saul was refreshed, and was well, and the evil spirit departed from him." Even today, we find that Christian music is extremely powerful in its ability to remove all evil presences from our environments. I highly recommend that you play Christian music consistently. Christian music will uplift your spirit, it will enhance your mood, and it will create a wonderful atmosphere in which to pray. Christian music also attracts the very presence of God and brings you to a better position to communicate effectively with God.

PRAISE AND WORSHIP

One of the first steps in prayer is to determine who to pray for first. Instead of jumping to our wish list, we should realize that we are having a conversation with the God of the universe. We should spend time praising God for who he is. As the Lord of all lords, we should recall that Jesus said, "Thou shalt love the Lord thy God with all thy heart, and with all thy soul, and with all thy mind. This is the first and greatest Commandment" (Matthew 22:37–38). If we truly love God and put him first, then the first person to praise is God.

GIVE THANKS

A next step in prayer is to thank God for everything that we have. We must remind God that we remember. He appreciates it. Even the littlest things in life, such as finding a good parking place without effort or having a simple cup of coffee in the morning are items for which we should thank God. Sometimes, we just have to say the words. We must recognize that everything we have has come from God. Even the very breath of life that is within us has come from God. In Psalm 104:33, the Word states, "When you [God] give them your breath, life is created and you renew the face of the earth." We must also remember God gave his Son to die for us. Jesus informed us, "For God so loved the world that he gave his only begotten Son, that whosoever believeth in him shall not perish but have everlasting life" (John 3:16).

To make it personal, you can have a list of truly great things that God has done for you. You can personally thank God for the time he saved you from being hurt, the time he helped you pass your final exam, the finding of a spouse or loved one, the delivery of your first child, or the act of salvation. I personally have a list of miracles that are too numerous to count. But we all can begin somewhere. Begin thanking God for his grace. Even thanking him for a cup of water or a bed to sleep in can be given to our Lord in prayer. God loves the little things in life, and he appreciates that you give him thanks for even the little things. I always say, "That's the favor of God in my life." Thank you, God.

REMIND GOD OF HIS PROMISES

A third step before jumping into your wish list is to remind God of his promises. Doing so means that you believe that God is a faithful and loyal God. It means that you trust in him to deliver on what he has told you he was going to do. This gets to your faith. God wants you to exercise your faith. "Faith is the substance of things hoped for, the evident of things unseen" (Hebrews 11:1). Remember, for it is written, "But without faith it is impossible to please him [God], for he that cometh to God must believe that he is a rewarder of them that diligently think him" (Hebrews 11:6). Through prayer is our opportunity to ask for things that God has promised us, through our faith in our Lord. God loves faith. God respects faith. God rewards faith. He wants us to stretch, exercise, and use our faith in requesting things because it reminds him that we are using his Word to get things that he has promised.

EFFECTIVE HABIT #6

Practice the Habit of Prayer

THE EFFECTIVE HABIT OF PRAYER is an essential part of being a Christian. As newcomers, we must realize that there are important aspects of prayer that increase its power and effectiveness. We must also learn that effective prayer is a learned skill and that it takes time to mature and to manifest its power. Just like a boxer does not throw the knock-out punch on his first attempt, the nuances of effective prayer take time. Nonetheless, we must remember that it is mentioned in James 5:16 that "the effective prayer of a righteous man [or woman] availeth much." There are several basic keys to improving the effectiveness of prayer. A few are described below.

PRAY IN THE NAME OF JESUS

As new believers, we must realize that there is tremendous power in *the name of Jesus*. As Paul mentioned in James 2:17, "You believe that there is one God, you do well, the devils also believe and tremble." Just the use of the name of Jesus causes demons to tremble. Moreover, in Proverbs 18:10, the Word reminds us, "The Name of the Lord is a strong tower; the righteous run into it and are safe." Through experience, you will learn that praying with the words, "in the name of Jesus," will greatly magnify the power of your prayers and improve the outcome dramatically.

PRAY THROUGH JESUS—A PERFECT HIGH PRIEST—TO THE FATHER

In the Bible, the qualifications of the high priest were essential for prayers to be answered. If the high priest had a weakness or sin, then the prayers of Israel would not be answered. The tremendous difference that we have today is that Jesus is our great and perfect high priest. No one else in the world is as qualified as Jesus. No one else will ever be as qualified as Jesus. The Bible also confirms this assertion in Hebrews 4:14–15, when the apostles notify us that "we have *a great High Priest in Jesus.*" This "*High Priest* cannot be touched with the feeling of our infirmities; but was in all points tempted like as we are, yet without sin (emphasis mine)." Jesus was tested in every way possible, yet he came out of these tests without sin and perfect in the eyes of God. We must remember to ask for Jesus to intercede for our prayers as a righteous and perfect high priest.

THE POWER OF PRAYER WITH TWO OR MORE PEOPLE

One of the principles of prayer is that two people praying together are more powerful than just one person. We should note that Jesus even talked about this. Jesus stated in Matthew 18:20, "For where two or three are gathered in my Name, there am I, in the midst of them." Also, the Bible states, "Two are better than one; because they have a good reward for their labour. For if they fall, the one will lift up his fellow: but woe to him that is alone when he falleth; for he hath not another to help him up. Again, if two lie together, then they have heat: but how can one be warm alone? And if one prevail against him, two shall withstand him; and a threefold cord is not quickly broken" (Ecclesiastes 4:9–12). This reiterates the point, which is that Jesus encourages us to gather in prayer and, if possible, pray with two or more people.

This guidance above is for the new Christian. As a new Christian, it is often difficult to find someone to pray with you when you are first learning about the Christian faith. Also, it may not be easy to even talk about requesting prayer support, as you may not feel comfortable with asking these questions. I recommend that you consider joining a small group session at your local church that is devoted to learning about the Bible and to assisting new Christians. Also, you may consider joining a youth group that has a Christian focus or looking for a Bible study or prayer group within your church that encourages prayer in a group setting.

Group Prayer Is Quite Powerful

By meeting a group of Christians, you will have others to support you during times of trial. As a new Christian, trials will certainly occur as you begin to grow your faith in an environment that may work against your growth. The bible provides guidance to "Humble yourselves therefore under the mighty hand of God, that he may exalt you in due time. Casting all your care upon him; for he careth for you. Be sober, be vigilant; because your adversary the devil, as a roaring lion, walketh about, seeking whom he may devour" (1 Peter 5:6–9).

Pray with Confidence

When we come in prayer, Jesus wants us to be confident that our prayers will be answered. He encourages us to rest assured that those things we ask for shall come to us. Jesus informs us directly and states, "*Ask*, and it shall be given you; *seek*, and ye shall find; *knock,* and it shall be opened unto you. For every one that asketh receiveth; and he that seeketh findeth; and to him that knocketh it shall be opened" (Matthew 7:7–8).

Moreover, Jesus wants us to know that the Father truly cares about what we ask for. Jesus informs us, "Or what man is there of you, whom if his son ask bread, will he give him a stone? Or if he ask a fish, will he give him a serpent? If ye then, being evil, know how to give good gifts unto your children, how much more shall your Father which is in heaven give good things to them that ask him" (Matthew 7:9–11). To Jesus, it is utterly inconceivable that our heavenly Father will not respond to our requests when our earthly father readily gives us the things for which we ask.

Pray with Boldness

The Bible informs us that we need to act boldly when we pray. The book of Hebrews emphasizes the reasons that we should feel confident to act boldly. The apostles remind us the "word of God is quick, and powerful, and sharper than any two-edged sword, piercing even to the dividing asunder of soul and spirit, and of the joints and marrow, and is a discerner of the thoughts and intents of the heart" (Hebrews 4:12). Therefore, we are encouraged as Christians to "Let us therefore *come boldly unto the throne of grace,* that we may obtain mercy, and find grace to help in time of need" (Hebrews 4:16).

Pray with Strength and Firm Conviction

When we pray, we must do so with the firm belief that what we pray for will definitely be answered. To help us understand this habit, Jesus provided us with firm guidance. "For verily I say unto you, That whosoever shall say unto this mountain, Be thou removed, and be thou cast into the sea; and shall not doubt in his heart, but shall believe that those things which he saith shall come to pass; he shall have whatsoever he saith" (Mark 11:23). Additionally, he clarified this idea by noting, "Therefore I say unto you, what things soever ye desire, when ye pray, believe that ye receive them, and ye shall have them" (Mark 11:24). God is reminding us that prayers are effective and powerful when we truly believe that what we ask for will come to pass. We must believe in our hearts that the things we pray for will definitely happen. There is no hesitation in our prayer requests. There is no doubt in our hearts. Only when we have this firm conviction will prayers be answered on a regular basis.

PRAY WITH COMPASSION THROUGH A TIME OF BURDEN

At times, the Lord will place upon you a heavy burden to pray for someone or for some situation. His burden upon your prayer life indicates that something devastating or an important transition is underway. When this situation comes upon you, you should pray without ceasing until the burden is lifted. Anything short of this will not fulfill God's purpose during this period of burden. Ensure that you break the burden, and wait until the burden lifts. Pray until the weight lifts. The Bible informs us, "The burden of the word of the LORD for Israel, saith the LORD, which stretcheth forth the heavens, and layeth the foundation of the earth, and formeth the spirit of man within him" (Zechariah 12:1). We must be prepared to stand in the gap and to intercede for others until the burden is lifted.

PRAY OUT OF GRACE AND NOT OUT OF SELFISHNESS

When we come to God in prayer, we should make it a habit during our prayer session to ask God what he wants first. God should come first in all of our conversations with him. We should remember that the Bible states, *"Take delight in the Lord, and he will give you the desires of your heart"* (Psalms 37:4). This means that we need to gain a better understanding of what it takes to "delight" in the Lord and to learn how to please him. In many cases, he may expect us to make personal sacrifices that truly indicate to him that we are willing to invest in our relationships with the Lord. A personal sacrifice may mean moving to a new location where the Lord can bless us. Another sacrifice may be to quit a bad habit that is obstructing our relationships with God. Still another sacrifice may be taking the first step in getting rid of personal idols, such as things we haven't used for six months or longer. Sacrifice can come in many forms, but the important things is that we are giving up something to gain a closer relationship with the Lord.

PRAY WITH HUMBLENESS

One of the techniques that I have used in prayer is to first ask Jesus for forgiveness for all of my past sins. After recounting these sins of the past day, I ask for him to blot out all of my transgressions with the blood of Jesus. Routinely, I do this each day before prayer. The next step is to humble myself in front of God. I visualize that I am extremely small and literally shrinking into a little vessel, tiny in the sight of God, to let the Lord know that I am small in his sight. I ask the Lord, "Why should the God of the universe answer my prayers over and above all of the millions of people in the world who have severe conditions?" These conditions could be cancer, hospitalization, extreme poverty, or debilitating diseases. With this visualization, I realize that my prayer requests are extremely small in comparison to others and that I sincerely appreciate any attention that God may give to my humble request. From this position of smallness in God's sight, I have conditioned myself to truly desire the answer from the God of the universe. At that point, God has rewarded me for this preparation of bringing humility to my every prayer encounter.

God confirms this approach in by stating, "*Humble yourselves in the sight of the Lord*, and He will lift you up" (James 4:10). Additionally, the Bible informs us, "*Be clothed with humility* - for God resisteth the proud, and *giveth grace to the humble. Humble yourselves* therefore under the mighty hand of God, that he may exalt you in due time" (1 Peter 5:5–6). Moreover, God reveals, "If my people, which are called by my name, *shall humble themselves*, and pray, and seek my face, and turn from their wicked ways; then will I hear from heaven, and will forgive their sin, and will heal their land" (2 Chronicles 7:14). The rewards of humility, especially in prayer, are repeated throughout the Bible.

LEARN HOW TO "BE STILL" IN PRAYER

Often in prayer, we are unsettled and let the cares of the world distract us. To be truly effective in prayer, we must learn to place our cares upon the Lord. It is through his strength and his power that prayers will be answered. The advice that the Lord provides us is simple. Our Lord reminds us in prayer, "Be still, and know that I am God: I will be exalted among the heathen, I will be exalted in the earth" (Psalm 46:10). By reminding God of this promise, we will find peace and strength, and our prayers will be answered powerfully.

Motivation—Willingness to Change Our Behavior

BE CONVICTED BY THE HOLY SPIRIT

As NEW CHRISTIANS WE MUST be willing to change our behavior to move closer to God. In this regard, as we ask God for guidance on how to change ourselves, we should expect the Holy Spirit to convict us of our need for change. Change, if for better behaviors, is important. An example of the kinds of things of which the Holy Spirit corrects us are mentioned in Colossians 3:5–8. They include uncleanness, evil desires, covetousness, idolatry, disobedience, malice, wrath, anger, blasphemy, and filthy language. Also, scripture informs us, "Now the works of the flesh are manifest, which are these; Adultery, fornication, uncleanness, lasciviousness, idolatry, witchcraft, hatred, variance, emulations, wrath, strife, seditions, heresies, envyings, murders, drunkenness, revellings, and such like: of the which I tell you before, as I have also told you in time past, that they which do such things shall not inherit the kingdom of God" (Galatians 5:19–21).

The Bible lets us know that these are the fruits of the flesh.

Hence, if we are living in the world, we would display the types of behaviors mentioned above. We can tell what is in our hearts by the fruits of our behavior.

MODELING GOOD BEHAVIOR

To help us to improve our behavior, the Bible provides us with examples of how to model after Jesus. We can learn how to become more like Jesus Christ by understanding the fruit of the Spirit.

The apostle Paul notes, "But the fruit of the Spirit is love, joy, peace, longsuffering, gentleness, goodness, faith, meekness, temperance: against such there is no law. And they that are Christ's have crucified the flesh with the affections and lusts. If we live in the Spirit, let us also walk in the Spirit" (Galatians 3:22–25).

Calling in the Favor of God

DELIVERANCE FROM THE CURSE

THE APOSTLE PAUL PROVIDED ADVICE on how to be delivered from generational and family curses. In Galatians 3:13, it states, "Christ has redeemed us from the curse of the law, having become a curse from us. For it is written, cursed is everyone who hangs on a tree that the blessing of Abraham might come on the Gentiles in Christ Jesus, that we might receive the promise of the Spirit through faith."

What does this mean? Paul is revealing to us that we can transfer all of our sins and our curses upon Jesus Christ. It is possible because Jesus has already paid the price for all of our sins, iniquities, curses, sicknesses, and diseases by sacrificing his life on the cross. Your debts have been paid in full. As a result, we can now ask for the divine transfer. We can receive all of the blessings that Jesus Christ deserves; since Jesus has already received all of the sins and curses that we deserve. All we have to do is ask for the transfer.

CALLING IN THE FAVOR OF GOD

The favor of God is available to anyone who asks for it. The apostle Paul states, "If we belong to Christ, then are you Abraham's seed and a heir according to the promise" (Galatians 3:29). The promise to Abraham is described in Genesis 12:2 as, "I will bless you, I will make your name great, and I will bless you to be a blessing." The Amplified Bible translates "I will bless you to be a blessing" as "I will give you an abundant increase of favor." This favor of God is available to all of us. All we need to do is ask for this favor of God routinely, every morning, and we will reap the harvest of our prayers. We will recognize that the words we consistently speak will manifest in our lives, due to the power of our words.

EFFECTIVE HABIT #9

Establishing Protection
in Times of Trouble

IN OUR CHRISTIAN WALK, WE will find, at times, that we will need to pray for protection. Protection may be needed due to a number of distractions. In some cases, we may need to create an environment or atmosphere of protection from the distractions of life. Have you ever been afflicted by feelings and emotions that prevent you from praying effectively—feelings of anxiety, anxiousness, confusion, heaviness, oppression, or moodiness and depression? In other cases, we may feel physical oppression that prevents us from praying. At other times, spiritual blocks or demonic presences may provide real obstacles to prayer. The habits below may be the most effective means of reestablishing an atmosphere of protection that allows you to pray effectively.

PLAY CHRISTIAN MUSIC

The earliest example of the power of Christian music is David's playing the harp to ward off evil spirits from afflicting King Saul. In 1 Samuel 16:23, scriptures reveal, "And it came to pass, when the evil spirit from God was upon Saul, that David took an harp, and played with his hand: so Saul was refreshed, and was well, and the evil spirit departed from him." Even today, we find that Christian music is extremely powerful in its ability to remove all evil presences from our environment. Play Christian music consistently. Christian music will uplift your spirit, enhance your mood, and create a wonderful atmosphere in which to pray. Christian music also attracts the very presence of God and brings you to a better position to communicate effectively with God.

APPLY THE BLOOD OF JESUS

As many mature Christians will attest, there is true and compelling power in the blood of Jesus Christ. It was through his shed blood for the salvation of all humankind that has provided the overwhelming power to free each of us from the bondages of sin and death. When it comes to creating an atmosphere of protection, all we need to do is pray to apply the blood of Jesus to cover all of the spiritual blockages, demonic influences, and any and all obstructions that are affecting our prayer lives. With firm boldness, declare and decree that the blood of Jesus covers all spirits, all powers, all rulers of this present darkness, and all of the powers of darkness to remove all obstacles, all obstructions, and all hindrances that are affecting your prayers. This blood of Jesus, when applied in prayer, causes excruciatingly great pain and unspeakable suffering for those demonic influences that stand in the way of your effective prayers.

Coupled with applying the blood of Jesus, you can also use the name of the Lord as a source of protection. Proverbs 18:10 informs the new Christian that "the Name of the Lord is a strong tower; the righteous runneth into it, and is safe." You can decree that the name of the Lord is a place of refuge and, in prayer, state that the name of Jesus is a source of safety and provides protection from many forms of opposition and adversity.

PRAY FOR THE ARMOR OF GOD

The apostle Paul provides sound advice on how to protect ourselves from the many attacks in the world. He reminds us that we need to "Put on the whole armour of God, that ye may be able to stand against the wiles of the devil. For we wrestle not against flesh and blood, but against principalities, against powers, against the rulers of the darkness of this world, against spiritual wickedness in high places" (Ephesians 6:10–12). From this passage, Paul informs us that our challenges in the world are not just physical. He lets us know that we also war against spiritual adversaries in the form of "principalities, powers, rulers of the darkness and spiritual wickedness." By putting on the whole armor of God, we can mitigate the effects of spiritual attacks.

What is in the armor of God? These basic pieces of the armor of God can be prayed for. Paul comments, "Stand therefore, having your loins girt about with truth, and having on the breastplate of righteousness. And your feet shod with the preparation of the gospel of peace. Above all, taking the shield of faith, wherewith ye shall be able to quench all the fiery darts of the wicked. And take the helmet of salvation, and the sword of the Spirit, which is the word of God" (Ephesians 6:14–17).

PRAY FOR THE CIRCLE OF FIRE

As Christians, we can also pray for circles of protection to strengthen our defense against our spiritual adversaries. In 2 Kings 6:17, the prophet Elisha demonstrated to one of his servants that a circle of fire could be made possible when Elisha confronted the army of Syria in the town of Dothan. Elisha asked the Lord to open the eyes of his servant. The Bible states, "And Elisha prayed, and said, LORD, I pray thee, open his eyes, that he may see. And the LORD opened the eyes of the young man; and he saw: and, behold, the mountain was full of horses and chariots of fire round about Elisha" (2 Kings 6:17). As Christians, we too can pray for a circle of fire to surround us in our battles against the spiritual world.

PRAY FOR THE HEDGE OF PROTECTION

In the Old Testament, the book of Job revealed another form of protection that God created to protect his loyal servants from the attacks of Satan. Interestingly, it was Satan himself that revealed this information to the Christian community. In Job 1:9–11, the scriptures highlight this method:

> Then Satan answered the LORD, and said, Doth Job fear God for nought? Hast not thou made an hedge about him, and about his house, and about all that he hath on every side? thou hast blessed the work of his hands, and his substance is increased in the land. But put forth thine hand now, and touch all that he hath, and he will curse thee to thy face.

Only after God agreed to take down the hedge of protection was Satan allowed to touch Job and his possessions. Since Job was able to receive this hedge of protection, we, as Christians, also are entitled to ask for this form of protection.

PRAY FOR THE HEDGE OF THORNS

In the Old Testament, the prophet Hosea prayed for a hedge of thorns to protect his spouse from setbacks, adversity, and challenges. Over time, Hosea discovered that his spouse was guilty of infidelity and of leaving her home for the company of others. The prophet Hosea took his problem to the prayer room and asked for a specific solution to his problem. Hosea prayed, "Therefore, behold, I will hedge up thy way with thorns, and make a wall, that she shall not find her paths" (Hosea 2:6). Hosea anticipated the effectiveness of this hedge of thorns by noting that "she shall follow after her lovers, but she shall not overtake them; and she shall seek them, but shall not find them" (Hosea 2:7). In response to this hedge, Hosea prophesied that "shall she say, I will go and return to my first husband; for then was it better with me than now" (Hosea 2:7). By such a prayer, Hosea created a hedge of protection to protect his spouse from doing evil and to return her to a right relationship.

PRAY FOR PROTECTION IN THE SECRET PLACE

Psalm 91 is one of my favorite prayers for protection from all forms of adversity. Psalm 91:1 discusses the "secret place of the most High" where we can abide in the shadow of the almighty God. The secret place is a place of refuge. It is available for those who ask for it. In this secret place, no evil entity can find you, for through prayer you are concealed from those who seek you in the realm of the spirit. This Psalm 91 protection is available for all those who ask to be placed in this secret place. In my times of distress, praying the entire Psalm 91 has been highly effective in providing a layer of protection for me and my loved ones.

GAIN RELIEF FROM THE SPIRIT OF FEAR AND ANXIETY

When it comes to protection, we must remember that God does not intend for us to have any feelings of fear or anxiety. These feelings are not of God. If these feelings afflict you, I highly recommend that you pray, based on 2 Timothy 1:7, "For God hath not given us the spirit of fear; *but of power, and of love, and of a sound mind.*" You can use this prayer whenever you feel anxiousness coming on. God has the power to remove fear and anxiety. By simply praying the prayer in 2 Timothy 1:7, you will feel relief from those emotions. Additionally, you can pray consistently to apply the blood of Jesus to your emotions, and those feelings should melt away.

Changing Your Mind-Set

BECOMING CONFORMED TO GOD

ONE OF THE QUESTIONS WE must ask ourselves is, "Are we conformed to the world, or are we conformed to the image of God?" Habits are an indicator of to what we are conformed. As new Christians, we are on the pathway to transform ourselves from our present lives to lives that follow Christ. One of the first steps of a new Christian is to determine if we are conformed to the world. If so, how are we conformed to the world? At the heart of this search is asking ourselves the very basic question, "What do I value in life?" Early indicators of our habits should reveal what we value deeply within our hearts. For the Word says, "Keep your heart with all diligence, for out of the heart are the issues of life" (Proverbs 4:12).

As we study ourselves, we will learn more about what we truly value. Examples can be found by watching our behavior. Do we spend most of our days on the Internet and using our smartphone devices, or do we spend time communicating with God? When we use our smartphones, are we shopping for the latest great buys at our favorite online shopping network, or are we thinking about ways to serve others in our community? Do we post our latest pictures to Facebook or Instagram in order to boast about ourselves, or do we post items about Jesus to glorify God? Do we spend numerous hours watching our favorite TV sitcoms, or do we value quiet time in prayer, on reading the Word of God, or on spending time praising God? These are just a few examples of how a short study of our habits can give us an idea if we are conformed to the world ... or conformed to God.

Many people believe that they are Christians and, as a result, that they are basically "good" people. We all believe that we are good. Nobody wants to believe that he or she is not good. Interestingly, the average person in America believes that he or she is living a good life. We generally take care of all of our responsibilities, we pay our bills, we don't break any laws, we don't steal, we keep our yards clean, and we attend church at least once a week. People basically believe that they are good. And they believe that they will go to heaven because they have lived a so-called "good" life.

This is not exactly true. This firm personal belief does not match what the Word of God says in the Bible. The apostle Paul clarified God's Word by reminding us, "For all have sinned and fall short of the Glory of God; being justified freely by his Grace through the redemption that is in Christ Jesus" (Romans 3:23–24). What does this mean? It means that even though we believe that we are basically good, we all have sinned and thus have fallen short of meeting the most basic requirement for getting into heaven. We have sinned. We are sinners. And sinners can't get into heaven on their own. In essence, the only way that we, as sinners, can get to heaven is by being washed clean by the blood of Jesus. We need to have a daily walk with God and ask him for forgiveness of our sins daily.

This saying is a hard truth. Many of us are still in denial. Change is hard. Change is difficult. Change is uncomfortable. Change is unnatural. Let's face it; none of us wants to change. The truth is that we like our daily routines and staying in our comfort zones. We enjoy our daily routines of getting our first cup of coffee, listening to the news, hearing our favorite songs over the Internet, keeping our home temperature at seventy degrees, and having our morning cereal, yogurt, juice, or eggs. We like our morning commute to work and greeting our fellow workers at the office. Behind all of this, we are creatures of comfort, and these are our habits. It all gets back to habits. Unless we are willing to change our habits, we will be unwilling to change our path toward God.

To get on the right path, we must realize that it is all about our habits. We need to identify and establish fresh habits to seek God. Change will not come about easily, but change can come if we are willing to change our habits. This book is about seeking, finding, and using new habits of behavior to help us on the path toward finding God. It may not be easy, but it certainly will be easier.

REMOVE IDOLS IN YOUR LIFE

Many of us have great difficulty believing that we worship idols in our lives. The simplest way to point this out is to identify common idols that all humans may have. What is an idol? An idol is something that you love more than God. An idol can come in many forms. For those who love work more than anything else in life, their job can become an idol above their love of God. Examples of idols in your life could be personal mementos that you treasure above anything else, such as trophies of your championship victories that are a source of your own personal identity. Statues of key personalities that you treasure and worship above all other possessions are examples of idols. A collection of invaluable oil paintings that you feel that you cannot give away or remove from your house can be a source of idols. Valuable name-brand clothing and expensive diamond jewelry can be a source of idols and something that you love more than God himself. Even something as simple as family photographs that you cannot live without can quickly become a personal idol that stands between you and God and also stands between you and salvation.

YOU CANNOT SERVE GOD AND RICHES

An idol prevents you from serving God. The Bible reminds us, " No man can serve two masters: for either he will hate the one, and love the other; or else he will hold to the one, and despise the other. Ye cannot serve God and mammon" (Matthew 6:24). As you continue your walk with the Lord, you will find that God will expect you to get rid of anything in your life that has a higher priority than him. One by one, you will see God stripping away those things that you value most in life and what may be considered before God. Also, the Bible states, "Keep yourselves from Idols" (1 John 5:21).

In short, we must realize that an idol can be virtually anything in our lives that we have in our hearts above our Creator. The list of idols is only limited by our imagination. Let's face it; many of us have scores of idols, and we don't even realize it. The only way to truly identify our idols is to ask the Holy Spirit to reveal them to us. This realization may be difficult, but we must take the first step in getting rid of all of our idols so that we can serve God only and God alone.

LEARN TO DO GOOD TO PLEASE GOD

What does this mean? When we do service for others, is this motivated by our personal desire to look good in front of others, or are we motivated to do good for God? Are we boasting to gain more respect from our neighbors? Are we striving to acquire trophies or medals or rewards for our walls? Do we seek recognition from others so that we can gain a faster promotion or a better office location? Or is it simply just about our pride in accomplishment? In all of these cases, we should check ourselves so that we are doing true service for God.

Jesus reminds us,

> Take heed that you do not do you charitable deeds before men, to be seen by them. Otherwise you have no reward from your father in heaven. Therefore, when you do a charitable deed, do not sound a trumpet before you as the hypocrites to in the synagogues and in the streets, that they may have glory from them. Assuredly, I say to you, they have their reward. But when you do a charitable deed, do not let your left hand know what the right hand is doing, that you charitable deed may be in secret and your father who sees in secret will Himself reward you openly. (Matthew 6:4)

LEARN TO LAY UP TREASURES IN HEAVEN

Where are your treasures? Are you working hard to save a financial nest egg for a comfortable retirement? Are you investing in your personal relationships with your neighbors so that they admire and respect you in your community? Are you collecting beautiful paintings and artwork so that visitors stand in awe of your collections? Jesus said, "Do not lay up for yourself treasures on earth where moth and rust destroy and where thieves break in and steal. But lay up for yourselves treasures in heaven, where neither moth nor rust destroy and where thieves do not break in and steal. For where your treasure is, there your heart will be also" (Matthew 6:19–20).

How do we lay up treasures in heaven? It is probably the opposite of what we believe. Jesus stated, "He that layeth up treasure for himself, ... is not rich toward God" (Luke 12:21). Then, you might ask, what do we need to do to store up treasure in heaven? Jesus replied to his disciples, "Sell what you have, and give alms [to the poor]; provide yourselves bags which wax not old, [store up] a treasure in the heavens that faileth not, where no thief approacheth, neither moth corrupteth." (Luke 12:33) He also reminded us, "For where your treasure is, there will your heart be also." (Matthew 6:21) In retrospect, we have too much. Many of us have tremendous luxuries that we don't even use. Yet there are many people living on the streets without even the most basic needs for themselves.

Jesus also provides advice on how to do good deeds in the proper way. Our intent or motivation for doing a good deed is also important to God. If we perform good deeds for our personal pride or reputation, we must realize that we are not getting credit for those good deeds, and we may not be laying up treasures in heaven. As Jesus reminds us,

> Take heed that you do not do your charitable deeds before men, to be seen by them. Otherwise you have no reward from your Father in heaven. Therefore, when you do a charitable deed, do not sound a trumpet before you as the hypocrites

do in the synagogues and in the streets, that they may have glory from men. Assuredly, I say to you, they have their reward. But when you do a charitable deed, do not let your left hand know what your right hand is doing, that your charitable deed may be in secret; and your Father who sees in secret will Himself reward you openly. (Matthew 6:1–4)

BE COMFORTABLE CONFESSING CHRIST BEFORE MAN

One of our habits as new Christians is to remember the importance of confessing Jesus before others. In fact, if you truly love Jesus, you will not be ashamed of him and will be open and willing to share your love for him. Jesus himself talks about the importance of this habit in Matthew 10:32, when he tells his disciples, "Whosoever therefore shall confess me before men, him will I confess also before my Father which is in heaven." In this regard, Jesus lets us know that there are personal rewards for those who are willing to share Jesus's story and confess him before men. Additionally, Jesus provided us with a warning when he stated, "But whosoever shall deny me before men, him will I also deny before my Father which is in heaven" (Matthew 10:33). Nevertheless, if you are a true Christian filled with the Holy Spirit, it should not be difficult for you to confess Jesus. The Bible states "that every tongue should confess that Jesus Christ is Lord, to the glory of God the Father" (Philippians 2:22). If you truly belong to Christ, it will be a natural act to make this confession."

LEARN TO GIVE GOD THE GLORY

God expects us to give him the glory in all things that we do. We must remember that all of creation points toward God's glory and reveals to man the grace of the Father. Even the creation of a blind man was to serve God's purpose of revealing his glory. The Bible tells us, "As he [Jesus] went along, he saw a man blind from birth. His disciples asked him, 'Rabbi, who sinned, this man or his parents, that he was born blind?' 'Neither this man nor his parents sinned,' said Jesus, 'but this happened so that the works of God might be displayed in him'" (John 9:1–3). Thus, the scriptures show us that even the birth of a man born blind can serve the purpose of revealing God's glory through a miracle of Jesus.

WE CAN GIVE GOD THE GLORY IN MANY WAYS

Too often we attribute miracles in our lives to our own works. How often have we boasted about a wonderful performance as a musician, our great speeches at graduation, or our recognition while volunteering at the local church as our own great deeds? We are very good at sounding our own trumpets. But how often have we attempted to give God the credit or to give God the glory. We often overlook this possibility and don't give credit where credit is due. God knows everything. Jesus reminds us,

> Take heed that you do not do your charitable
> deeds before men, to be seen by them. Otherwise
> you have no reward from your Father in heaven.
> Therefore, when you do a charitable deed, do
> not sound a trumpet before you as the hypocrites
> do in the synagogues and in the streets, that

they may have glory from men. Assuredly, I say to you, they have their reward. But when you do a charitable deed, do not let your left hand know what your right hand is doing, that your charitable deed may be in secret; and your Father who sees in secret will Himself reward you openly. (Matthew 6:1–4)

Choice and Obedience

THE ENTIRE CHRISTIAN WALK IS about choices. We make choices every day that affect our Christian lives. The habit of firsts, the habit of tithing, and the habit of prayer all involve making choices with our time and our thoughts. One of the most important choices that we can make is to develop the habit of obedience. You will find that it carries many blessings.

As new Christians, we must learn the value of obedience to the Father. Throughout the Bible, there are examples of how obedience was rewarded to those who chose to follow God's instructions. It also was evident that those who did not follow God's instructions received severe punishments when these choices were made. The stark differences between choosing obedience and choosing disobedience were highlighted in Deuteronomy 28. The following promises are a series of blessings to those Christians who obey God's Word. They include:

- "And it shall come to pass, if thou shalt hearken diligently unto the voice of the LORD thy God, to observe and to do all his commandments which I command thee this day, that the LORD thy God will set thee on high above all nations of the earth."(Deuteronomy 28:1)

- "And all these blessings shall come on thee, and overtake thee, if thou shalt hearken unto the voice of the LORD thy God."
- "Blessed shalt thou be in the city, and blessed shalt thou be in the field."
- "Blessed shall be the fruit of thy body, and the fruit of thy ground, and the fruit of thy cattle, the increase of thy kind, and the flocks of thy sheep."
- "Blessed shall be thy basket and thy store."
- "Blessed shalt thou be when thou comest in, and blessed shalt thou be when thou goest out."
- "The LORD shall cause thine enemies that rise up against thee to be smitten before thy face: they shall come out against thee one way, and flee before thee seven ways."
- "The LORD shall command the blessing upon thee in thy storehouses, and in all that thou settest thine hand unto; and he shall bless thee in the land which the LORD thy God giveth thee."
- "The LORD shall establish thee an holy people unto himself, as he hath sworn unto thee, if thou shalt keep the commandments of the LORD thy God, and walk in his ways."
- "And all people of the earth shall see that thou art called by the name of the LORD; and they shall be afraid of thee."
- "And the LORD shall make thee plenteous in goods, in the fruit of thy body, and in the fruit of thy cattle, and in the fruit of thy ground, in the land which the LORD sware unto thy fathers to give thee."

- "The LORD shall open unto thee his good treasure, the heaven to give the rain unto thy land in his season, and to bless all the work of thine hand: and thou shalt lend unto many nations, and thou shalt not borrow."
- "And the LORD shall make thee the head, and not the tail; and thou shalt be above only, and thou shalt not be beneath; if that thou hearken unto the commandments of the LORD thy God, which I command thee this day, to observe and to do them."
- "And thou shalt not go aside from any of the words which I command thee this day, to the right hand, or to the left, to go after other gods to serve them."

EFFECTIVE HABIT #12

Learning How to Deal with Trials and Temptations

TRIALS AND TEMPTATIONS ARE A part of the Christian walk. We should realize that all of us will face trials and temptations at some point in our lives. Even Jesus was not exempt. After he received the Holy Spirit, he was led into the desert to be tested for forty days. After having starved for many days, Satan tempted Jesus with the promise of food, the test of personal protection, and the promise of giving him all of the kingdoms of the world. In all cases, Jesus used the Word of God to rebuke Satan and to resist the multiple forms of temptation. You too will be tested and will undergo trials after you receive the Holy Spirit. Don't be surprised when these tests come; they are inevitable. The words in this book will help you to prepare for these trials.

DON'T LET SATAN STEAL YOUR JOY

As we begin to get closer to the Holy Spirit, Satan will get more involved with trying to undermine our Christian growth and development. Satan will search for our great vulnerabilities and try to exploit these vulnerabilities to cause us to question our faith. Often we can identify the form of Satan's attack by the emotions or feelings from which we are suffering at the time. For example, if we begin to feel depressed, it might be Satan's attack to paralyze our prayer lives or to pull our anchors away from Jesus. In these circumstances, we must learn to work with another Christian partner to help identify the attacks and to help us in prayer to counter the works of the devil. We must remember that we have the tools to accomplish this freedom from Satan. As God reminds us, "Ye are of God, little children, and have overcome them; because greater is he that is in you, than he that is in the world" (1 John 4:4). This passage tells us that the power of the Holy Spirit in us is more powerful than any spiritual power in the world. We must remember this position of superiority whenever we encounter difficulties in our prayer lives.

Learning How to Test the Spirits

As we begin to get stronger in our prayer lives, we will encounter new obstacles, new resistance, and even new spiritual voices. When we are challenged by new spiritual voices, God has given us a means to "test the spirits." The bible provides us with sound guidance on how to deal with such situations. The Word states,

> Beloved, believe not every spirit, but try the spirits whether they are of God: because many false prophets are gone out into the world. Hereby know ye the Spirit of God: Every spirit that confesseth that Jesus Christ is come in the flesh is of God. And every spirit that confesses not that Jesus Christ is come in the flesh is not of God; and this is that spirit of antichrist, whereof ye have heard that it should come; and even now already is it in the world. (1 John 4:1–3)

Learn the Power of the Tongue

ONE OF THE MOST IMPORTANT habits that we can perfect is the use of the tongue. As new Christians, we must be aware that everything we say is very powerful. The tongue is one of the smallest parts of the body, yet it carries tremendous weight when it comes to our direction in life. The scriptures tell us, "Behold, we put bits in the horses' mouths, that they may obey us; and we turn about their whole body" (James 3:3). Moreover, it notes, "Behold also the ships, which though they be so great, and are driven of fierce winds, yet are they turned about with a very small helm, whithersoever the governor listeth" (James 3:4). Smallness should not be equated with littleness. Our tongues can be the most powerful instruments we have in our possession.

Salvation comes from the power of the tongue. The Bible provides instruction on what it takes to gain salvation. In Romans 10:9–10, God's instruction states, "If you confess with your mouth the Lord Jesus and believe in your heart that God has raised Him from the dead, you will be saved. For with the heart one believes unto righteousness, and with the mouth confession is made unto salvation."

God created the heavens and the earth through the power of the tongue. In the very beginning, the first words that God spoke in Genesis 1:3 were, "Let there be light; and there was light." God then saw the light and saw that it was good. Throughout the first book of the Bible, God created the firmaments, the water, the vegetation, the seasons, the stars, the living creatures, and even humans through the power of the tongue. In all of this, we must remember that God used words to establish all of creation.

Death and life is determined by our tongues. Proverbs 18:21 reminds us, "Death and life are in the power of the tongue, and those who love it will eat its fruit." What power resides in our words? Is it possible that the tongue has that kind of power over our very lives? Additionally, the Bible tells us, "Even so the tongue is a little member, and boasteth great things. Behold, how great a matter a little fire kindleth!" (James 3:5–6).

The tongue is difficult to control. The book of James highlights that every other creature on earth has the potential to be tamed. Yet can the human tongue be tamed? The Bible notes, "For every kind of beasts, and of birds, and of serpents, and of things in the sea, is tamed, and hath been tamed of mankind ... But the tongue can no man tame; it is an unruly evil, full of deadly poison" (James 3:7–8).

With this perspective, it is evident that controlling our words and controlling our tongues can be a difficult proposition. Further, the Bible tells us "the tongue is a fire, a world of iniquity: so is the tongue among our members, that it defileth the whole body, and setteth on fire the course of nature; and it is set on fire of hell" (James 3:6). Wow, with this kind of perspective, we must be aware of the tremendous danger that resides in the use of the tongue.

The cleanliness of a man is determined by the power of the

tongue. As Jesus reminds us, "Not what goes into the mouth defiles a man; but what comes out of the mouth, this defiles a man" (Matthew 5:11). Hence, we do not sin by what we eat, but we can definitely sin by what we confess with our mouths. Jesus repeats himself in Matthew 5:18 by stating, "But those things which proceed out of the mouth come from the heart, and they defile a man." With this understanding, we can truly prevent ourselves from sinning by controlling the words that come from our lips.

The Holy Spirit has the power to control our tongues. By ourselves, we are unable to control the words that come from our mouths. Even though our intentions may be good, we basically lack the power and ability to control our own speech. Nevertheless, we can ask the Holy Spirit to intervene on our behalf and to apply his power to control our speech. In Psalm 141:3, the Bible teaches us to say, "Lord, set a guard over my mouth, Lord, keep watch over the door of my lips." Through prayer to the Holy Spirit, we can ask God to guide our words, place a guard over our mouths, and to oversee the door of our lips. In prayer, we should remind God—in accordance with the scriptures in Matthew 19:26, Mark 10:27, Luke 1:37, and Luke 18:28—"With man it is impossible, but with God all things are possible."

Find an Intercessor

INTERCESSORS ARE PEOPLE WHO ARE designated by God to pray for others. The scriptures tell us, "Confess *your* trespasses to one another, and pray for one another, that you may be healed. The effective, fervent prayer of a righteous man avails much" (James 5:16). Certain people have developed a refined skill of praying. They have established habits of consistent behavior that help them to intercede for others. God tells us that these prayer warriors are very powerful and effective in their undertakings. Thus, you can benefit greatly by finding a prayer intercessor at your local church to pray on your behalf.

Develop a Covenant with the Lord

GOD IS A GOD OF covenants. Throughout the Bible, there are numerous stories of how God made covenants with key individuals who became great men and women of faith. Abraham made a covenant with God very early in his walk. A key to having God make a covenant with you is to be obedient. Abraham was obedient in all things that the Lord asked him to do. The Bible tells us of God's instructions to Abraham. After his father passed away, God came to Abram (his earlier name) and told him, "Get out of your country, from your family, and from your father's house, to a Land that I will show you" (Genesis 12:1). If he was obedient, God promised Abram, "I will make you a great nation. I will bless you and make your name great. And you shall be a blessing. I will bless those who bless you, and I will curse him who curses you; and in you all the families of the earth shall be blessed" (Genesis 12:2–3).

With this instruction, Abram was obedient to God. He left his country and departed to the land where God told him to go. In return, God made a covenant with Abram and, as long as Abram remained obedient, God honored and blessed this covenant.

What is a covenant? From the Bible, we learn that a covenant is a sacred agreement between God and an individual or a group of people. God provides certain conditions that must be met by the individual or the group of people. If we obey his conditions, God promises to bless us. When we purposely choose not to obey his conditions or his instructions, we do not receive God's blessings. In fact, in some cases we suffer a penalty, a punishment, or severe consequences as a result of any disobedience. Thus, the key to maintaining a covenant is to be obedient. If we study this condition, we will find that habits help us to keep our willpower and our condition of being obedient.

Why does God make covenants? God truly wants to have a personal relationship with humans. God invests in one person at a time. God desires intimacy. He truly loves us and wants us to get closer to him in truth and in spirit. A covenant is an approach to getting closer to God. A covenant creates an agreement between us and the sovereign God of the universe. How powerful is that? We can't get any more powerful that personal relationships with a sovereign deity. While this may seem impossible, it is a very real possibility for those who love God and are willing to make a sacrifice. Obedience to God's covenant agreement is not always easy, and it often requires deep personal sacrifice to make it work. The rewards are overwhelming, but the costs must be borne by the new Christian.

Living the Life of the Spirit

WHAT DOES IT MEAN TO live the life of the Spirit? In Romans 8:2, the apostle Paul tells us that if we are living the life of the Spirit, we basically are "free from the laws of sin and death." If we are living with the Spirit, we should not have a life that is filled with alcoholism, drugs, addictions, or anything of the sort. We must remember that those who live their lives according to the flesh basically set their minds on things of the flesh. In Colossians 3:5–8, the apostle Paul provides pertinent examples of living according to the flesh and reveals many of the bad habits of the flesh. These include such habits as fornication, lust, envy, idolatry, anger, wrath, malice, blasphemy, filthy language, and the like.

In contrast, the Bible also gives guidance on the fruits of the Spirit if we are living the life of the Spirit. In Colossians 3:12–17, the apostle Paul reveals many of the good habits associated with the life of the Spirit. These include such habits as mercies, kindness, humbleness, meekness, longsuffering, forgiveness, charity, peace, and giving thanks to God. From this discussion, it is evident that we can observe a person who is living the life of the Spirit by his or her personal behavior. The person's behavior is also called his or her "fruits."

To whom do we belong? The Bible tells us that we can tell the Lord that we serve, based on the Spirit. Paul tells us, "But you are not in the flesh but in the Spirit, if indeed the Spirit of God dwells in you. Now if anyone does not have the Spirit of Christ, he is not His" (Romans 8:9). Thus, Paul reminds us that to be a part of Jesus Christ and the Father, we must have the Spirit of God indwelling within us. Romans 8:14 states, "For as many as are led by the Spirit of God, these are sons of God."

Likewise, it is also possible to tell if we are not of Jesus Christ and the Father. The Bible tell us, "For to be carnally minded *is* death, but to be spiritually minded *is* life and peace. Because the carnal mind *is* enmity against God; for it is not subject to the law of God, nor indeed can be. So then, those who are in the flesh cannot please God" (Romans 8:6). Hence, again we can tell to whom we belong by serving our habits, our behaviors, and our fruits that are either of the flesh or of God.

Learning to Have a Positive Attitude and Mind-Set

EVERYTHING IN THIS WORLD COMES from either a positive source or a negative source. In simple terms, our positive feelings and mind-sets come from God, our Father. The opposite, or negative feelings and mind-sets, come from Satan. These two opposing thoughts, mind-sets, and feelings are constantly in conflict throughout our daily lives. Our thoughts are constantly bombarded with ideas that tend toward positive outcomes or are bombarded with lies that lead to negative outcomes. Once we gain awareness of this constant struggle in our minds, we can choose a path of positivity that truly leads to God.

POSITIVE THOUGHTS ARE A HABIT OF CHOICE

Every day we are confronted with some small challenge. These challenges could come in the form of cutting ourselves while shaving, stubbing our toes on a corner, slipping and falling on a wet floor, or having a bad hair day. All of these small things happen to everyone and are natural. However, the choice of what to think or how to reflect on these challenges is based on our own personal habits. We can choose to pout, to be gloomy, or to spout numerous expletives. On the other hand, we can choose to replace thoughts of negativity with our own personal habit of positive thoughts.

The Bible tells us, "Do all things without complaining and grumbling, that you may become blameless and harmless, children of God without fault in the midst of a crooked and perverse generation, among whom you shine as lights in the world" (Philippians 2:14). Moreover, the scriptures also tell us, "Finally, brethren, whatsoever things are true, whatsoever things are honest, whatsoever things are just, whatsoever things are pure, whatsoever things are lovely, whatsoever things are of good report; if there be any virtue, and if there be any praise, think on these things" (Philippians 4:8).

ELIMINATE WORRY AND FEAR

We must realize that worry is not a part of God's kingdom. In 2 Timothy 1:7, God reminds us, "For God hath not given us the spirit of fear; but of power, and of love, and of a sound mind." From this passage, we must recognize that *fear* and *worry* are spirits. As spirits, they influence and affect new Christians who do not recognize what fear and worry actually are. It is only when we realize that these emotions and feelings are spiritual and not of God that we know how to deal with these spirits. We can call upon the Holy Spirit to remove these spirits of fear, worry, and anxiety that affect and influence us. We also can apply the blood of Jesus on these spirits, and they will go away. The Bible reminds us to "Only fear the LORD, and serve him in truth with all your heart: for consider how great things he hath done for you" (1 Samuel 12:24).

Do Not Entertain Worry

The other aspect of addressing fear, worry, and anxiety is that we must learn how to rid our minds of these spirits. Without a doubt, these spirits usually will return after a while. It is at those moments that we must learn to focus on positive things. Remember, God, through the Holy Spirit, has given us a spirit of power, love, and a sound mind. We must call upon the Lord to apply these spirits and to focus our minds on Jesus.

Through prayer, we can call upon the Lord to deliver us from these spirits. Through prayer, we can ask the Holy Spirit to fill us with thoughts of peace, love, and joy. In Philippians 4:7, the apostle Paul tells us, "The peace of God, which passeth all understanding, shall keep your hearts and minds through Christ Jesus." Also, Paul tells us how to focus our minds. He says, "Finally, brethren, whatsoever things are true, whatsoever things are honest, whatsoever things are just, whatsoever things are pure, whatsoever things are lovely, whatsoever things are of good report; if there be any virtue, and if there be any praise, think on these things" (Philippians 4:8).

Learn the Power of God's Calling According to God's Purpose

WE MUST RECOGNIZE THAT GOD has tremendous power in his calling placed upon individuals. Those whom God has chosen are predestined to glory. The apostle Paul tells us, "For those God foreknew he also predestined to be conformed to the image of his Son, that he might be the firstborn among many brothers and sisters. And those he predestined, he also called; those he called, he also justified; those he justified, he also glorified" (Romans 8:29–30).

The Bible also tells us, "He chose us in Him before the foundation of the world, that we should be holy and without blame before Him in love, having predestined us to adoption as sons by Jesus Christ to Himself, according to the good pleasure of His will, to the praise of the glory of His grace, by which He made us accepted in the Beloved" (Ephesians 1:4–6).

EFFECTIVE HABIT #20

Recognize the Blessings of the Firstborn

WE MUST RECOGNIZE THAT THE firstborn have a special place in God's eyes. The Bible tells us, "But he shall acknowledge the son … *as* the firstborn by giving him a double portion of all that he has, for he *is* the beginning of his strength; the right of the firstborn *is* his" (Deuteronomy 21:17). Moreover, those that receive the calling and are the eldest in the family have a responsibility to teach others within the family. Romans 9:12 tells us, "It was said unto her, The elder shall serve the younger." As the firstborn, these unique individuals are expected to serve their younger siblings.

EFFECTIVE HABIT #21

Be a Lamp to Others

ONE OF THE HABITS THAT we must learn to perfect is to be a light to the world. God does not want us to perfect ourselves just for ourselves; he wants us to show others how to be giving, loving, and a good neighbor to those around us. Jesus provides his thoughtful guidance by saying to his apostles, "You are the light of the world. A city that is set on a hill cannot be hidden. Nor do they light a lamp and put it under a basket, but on a lampstand, and it gives light to all *who are* in the house. Let your light so shine before men, that they may see your good works and glorify your Father in heaven" (Matthew 5:14–15). Hence, we are not being perfected only for ourselves but to shine upon the world and to give glory to God.

The Habit of Believing

In all that we do, we must believe that God is telling us the truth. Hebrews 6:18 reminds us that God's Word is true because "it is impossible for God to lie." Moreover, Jesus reminds us that "heaven and earth will pass away, but my words will never pass away" (Matthew 24:35). There are rewards for believing that God is telling the truth. Jesus specifically promises, "Therefore I say to you, whatever things you ask when you pray, believe that you receive *them,* and you will have *them*" (Mark 11:24). We must realize that everything that comes to pass is dependent upon our belief in God's promises.

EFFECTIVE HABIT #23

The Habit of Association

NEW CHRISTIANS MUST BE AWARE that our associations play a significant role on we will become. Our closest friends, relatives, and associates affect our thoughts, self-esteem, and even our decisions. Thus, as new Christians, we must be selective in the new group of associates, now that we have made a decision to follow Jesus Christ. The Bible tells us, "No immoral, impure or greedy person—such a person is an idolater—has any inheritance in the kingdom of Christ and of God. Let no one deceive you with empty words, for because of such things God's wrath comes on those who are disobedient. *Therefore do not be partners with them*" (Ephesians 5:5).

The scriptures provide guidance on the need to be careful with those closest to us. The Bible states, "He who walks with wise men shall be wise, but a companion of fools will be destroyed" (Proverbs 13:20). Moreover, the scriptures reminds us, "Make no friendship with an angry man; and with a furious man do not go. Lest you learn his ways, and get a snare for your soul" (Proverbs 22:24–25). Research has proven that our close friends, over time, will have a decisive part to play in shaping our behaviors, habits, and decisions.

The Habit of the Fear of the Lord

YOU MAY WONDER, "WHY DO I need to fear the Lord?" Many new Christians don't realize that the Bible is filled with numerous blessings that come upon those who truly fear the Lord. King Solomon claims, "In the fear of the LORD is strong confidence—and his children shall have a place of refuge. The fear of the LORD is a fountain of life, to depart from the snares of death" (In Proverbs 14:26–27). In the Bible, we find that the fear of the Lord brings protection. It creates a place of safe refuge, and it can even keep us away from an untimely death.

Moreover, King Solomon tells us, "The fear of the LORD is the beginning of wisdom: and the knowledge of the holy is understanding" (Proverbs 9:10). Who would have thought that gaining wisdom begins with this? Most of us might have thought that reading the Bible gives us wisdom. But God is telling us that the true secret to gaining wisdom is to fear him. Also, Proverbs 1:7 states, "The fear of the LORD is the beginning of knowledge, but fools despise wisdom and instruction." Besides wisdom, the fear of the Lord also leads to the gaining of knowledge. The Bible informs us, "The secret of the LORD *is* with those who fear Him, and He will show them

His covenant" (Psalms 25:14). Wow! We can even learn the secret of the Lord through fear of him, and those who follow this instruction will have the covenant revealed to them.

Last, King Solomon informs us that the fear of the Lord can even lengthen our life spans. The Bible states, "The fear of the Lord prolongs days, but the years of the wicked will be shortened" (Proverbs 10:27). Additionally, it states, "For by me thy days shall be multiplied, and the years of thy life shall be increased" (Proverbs 9:11).

In summary, who can resist the benefits of fearing the Lord? If we simply obey and follow God's instructions, we have the definite potential to receive extraordinary protection, uncommon wisdom, and the remarkable health of living a long life.

CONCLUSION

Effective habits are basic elements of an approach to establish a new and fresh pathway to get closer to God. They are the first steps for the new Christian who is experiencing difficulty with finding out more about the new walk with our Lord. Instead of relying upon others, new Christians can enjoy this experience within the comfort of their own homes. *The Effective Habits of a Newborn Christian* provides a simple step-by-step guide that is intended to help the new believer get started in being obedient to the Lord.

The most important step in this book is learning to forgive. Forgiveness is hard. Forgiveness requires a sacrifice. It will require you to step into an uncomfortable spot where you must rely upon a sovereign God to deliver you. Without doubt, if you do this, you will experience a tremendous relief and lifting of all of your burdens. Forgiving those who have hurt you the most and allowing Jesus to then forgive you of all of your sins is the most critical step in establishing your path to freedom and salvation. If you speak it and believe it, Jesus will truly deliver you.

Relationships are extremely important in the early stages of a newborn Christian. I am a firm believer in the need to establish *a personal one-on-one relationship* between a new

Christian and our God. Once you begin this walk with God, you will find how overwhelming God's response will be when he starts to work in your unique situations. I highly recommend that you *give God an opportunity to work in your life.*

THE SINNER'S PRAYER

Dear God,

I know that I am a sinner, and I ask for your forgiveness.

I believe that Jesus Christ is your Son. I believe that he died for my sins and that you raised him to life.

I want to trust Jesus as my Savior and follow him as Lord from this day forward. Guide my life and help me to do your will.

Please, Holy Spirit, come into my heart now and cleanse me. I pray this in the name of Jesus. Amen.

THE SERENITY PRAYER

Lord, grant me the serenity to accept the things I cannot change, the courage to change the things I can, and the wisdom to know the difference.

WORSHIP SONGS FOR NEW CHRISTIANS

- "Forever" by Kari Jobe
- "No Longer Slaves" by Bethel
- "It Is Well" by Bethel
- "I Surrender" by Hillsong
- "Still" by Hillsong
- "Redeemed" by Big Daddy Weave
- "My Story" by Big Daddy Weave
- "Overwhelmed" by Big Daddy Weave
- "Holy Spirit" by Francesca Battistelli
- "Rooftops" by Jesus Culture
- "I Give You My Heart" by Hillsong
- "Oceans" by Hillsong
- "Broken Vessels (Amazing Grace)" by Hillsong
- "Lord, I Offer My Life to You" by Don Moen
- "On My Knees" by Jaci Velasquez
- "I Don't Deserve You" by Plumb
- "Lord, I'm Ready Now" by Plumb

Printed in the United States
By Bookmasters